Leading Ladies

Leading Ladies

30 Tips for Dynamic Female Leaders

Linda Spalla

Over the Transom Publishing Company
Fairhope, Alabama
2003

Over the Transom Publishing Company
9 N. Church Street
Fairhope, AL 36532

Leading Ladies: 30 Tips for Dynamic Female Leaders
Copyright © 2003 by Linda Spalla
www.lindaspalla.com

Library of Congress Control Number: 2003103397
ISBN 0-9728930-0-8

Manufactured in the United States of America

Typeset in President and Palatino Linotype
Design and composition by
Suzanne S. Barnhill, Words into Type
Cover design by MaryLou Hyland

First Edition 2003
10 9 8 7 6 5 4 3 2 1

To Katharine,
who once told me to
"stop acting like a woman!"

Preface

This is a book about women as leaders. The generalizations made here regarding gender differences give existence and identity to this book. I have worked with so many smart, caring, effective men in my career, and I have worked with some egotistical, brownnosing jerks. To all the dynamic male colleagues who toiled with me side by side over twenty-five years, I want to underscore that your input in my success was significant. Instead of giving offense, I hope this book makes you more aware of your own leadership skills. To Craig, Bill S., Bill A., Stan, Dick, Bobby, Steve, Keith, Carver, Lee…a forever thanks. And to Nonda, Dawn, Holly, Terry…we gals made the men look good!

To lead like a Woman is...
To express...
To nurture...
To tend...
To mend...
To care...
To fulfill...
To bear...
To blend...
To inspire...
To mentor others on their journey.

Contents

Chapter 1

So You Want to
Be a Leader?

Introduction

What if I told you that in the hour or so it will take you to read this book I will dispel every notion you ever had about being female in the workplace? What if I could show you a more natural leadership path than the one you're presently on? What if I told you that women's leadership skills have just begun to be understood? Or that your femininity (despite what you've been told) is your best asset! Wouldn't you be curious?

This book is for women who wish to be dynamic leaders, whether of a company, a team, a country, or a cause. We're not talking management duties here. We're talking leadership, a thin spot of real estate where no one else is telling you which decision to make, where no one else is taking the blame, where no one else is cleaning up your messes, where no one else is sticking his or her neck out as far as yours, and where no one else is forging the vision. The kind of leadership this book divines requires that you put on a brand-new coat, that you fly at thirty thousand feet where the perspective is wide and breathtaking, that you prepare for a lonely journey, and that you expend the ultimate effort in emotional maturity. If you are female and want to be a dynamic leader, this book is for you.

Being open to new ideas is what we women do best. We are always in the fire, remaking ourselves. It would seem that men, God bless them, come into the world forged as pure steel. Their strength, though very appealing and very necessary at times, can put their leadership potential in jeopardy. But we're not here to discuss or bash men who lead. We're here to make a difference in *your* leadership style. We're here to help reshape your potential. I promise you that these thirty steps *do* work very successfully. They are simple, but far from easy. If you're a skeptic, try them on a dare! What have you got to lose?

This book is not politically correct by the standards of corporate America. It is not meant to advance my career or impress anyone. I am retired! *I will say things here that women have been screaming to say out loud for a decade or more.* This book is about setting you free…free to lead, free to be the women you are in the workplace. The message is simple: You don't have to abandon or even curb your femininity; you don't have to dress in drab business suits; you don't have to "think like a man." You can even smile and wear bright lipstick.

If the genderless maze of corporate persuasion has driven you a little crazy, I'm about to give you some peace of mind. Read on.

Genderless

In 1992, I became one of the few female CEOs of a television station in the country, and certainly the first in my particular broadcast group, owned by the New York Times Company. That year, I attended the CBS annual meeting in Los Angeles and found myself in a room with all white men…a large group of several hundred. I remember surveying the neatly aligned chairs, row by row, and counting maybe four or five other women. Eight years later in 2000, I attended the very same meeting, this time in Vegas, and the room was at least one-third women. Progress for the women's movement? Well, certainly, but also a keen awareness on the part of corporate America that women make excellent leaders. That proof has been in our performance and success. However, there's an unacknowledged piece to this success story: women make good leaders for the very reasons many refuse to admit—their femininity.

This point was underscored for me early on in my leadership journey. My boss denied my request to attend a seminar on women and stress in the workplace. (I was having lots of stress!) He said something to the effect that the company would never send me to a seminar that made a distinction for women. Furthermore, he went on to say that our company didn't have gender differences. They somehow, I guess, saw me as genderless. Wow! I certainly never saw myself that way. One doesn't argue with the big boss; I settled for his answer but with a twinge in my gut. I knew instinctively that something was wrong with that response; I was too new and too unsure of my position at the time to sort it out. But I never forgot his comment. With time, it all became clear to me.

There are gender differences; they are substantial. As women, those very feminine parts of our makeup can be tremendous assets to our success; in fact, they may be our most fertile opportunities if we pay attention!

Yes, Virginia, there are gender differences

Men and women lead differently because their chemical and physiological makeup is different. Read Dr. Joyce Brothers' book *What Every Woman Should Know About Men* if you don't believe me. I am *not* implying that women are better leaders; I am *not* implying that men are ineffective leaders. I am simply proposing that women can be dynamic leaders by using their feminine assets.

A picture is worth a thousand words. Think of two triangles, one with the base at the bottom in usual fashion (Figure 1). Label this one Male Leadership. Think of another that is turned on its end with the longer base line at the top and the point at the bottom (Figure 2). Label it Female Leadership. As you look at each figure, consider a paradigm shift: look at the usual, and then look at the usual from a totally different, refreshing perspective.

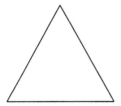 

Figure 1. Male Leadership   Figure 2. Female Leadership

A man leads from the top; he must be the "boss"; he must have a seat on his throne, his ivory tower in the sky, whatever you wish to call it. He can be very effective from that vantage point because it suits his nature. The caveat is that it takes everyone else to undergird him and hold the organization in place. A woman, on the other hand, is the pivotal defined point of the upside-down triangle; she is the foundation; she upholds the organization; she's more comfortable and more natural at the root position. She is, by her nature, the only gender who can bear fruit, if you will.

If you grasp this concept, it's obvious that one plays to the male ego, and the other plays to a woman's innate skill of providing a delicate balance of nurturing and equanimity. In Figure 2, the point of the triangle is the most fragile, the most vulnerable, and the most important for stability. It illustrates that a woman's energy can rise to the top, elevating her employees' contribution to a significance often overlooked by a man. It puts the efforts of the team above her individual effort. A man's forcefulness can sometimes sift to the bottom, potentially (not always) denting self-esteem and diminishing his employees' sense of worthiness to the company.

So much for triangles and paradigms and stereotypical generalizations. What, you may be asking about now, gives me the right to postulate such a position? How dare I presume to discuss leadership tips for other women? How dare I think I have an idea or two that might open new vistas for female leaders? These are fair questions. So before we go a step farther together, dear reader, let me share my story. How did a naïve little country gal from Anniston, Alabama, who had never flown in an airplane or been west of the Mississippi get to be the CEO and General Manager of a television station? How did she reach a point of maturity in her leadership skills and how did she learn to touch people's lives and make a difference? The bad news is that it wasn't easy or quick. But the good news is that if she could rise to the top, so can you!

My Story

In August of 1975, I divorced my first husband, left the home provided by his employer, the Methodist Church, and returned to Huntsville, Alabama. I was twenty-eight years old. I had only three things in my possession: a late-model Olds Cutlass, my houseplants, and my precious three-year old son, Christopher. The furniture, the insurance, the appliances, the social niceties all stayed with my ex, as did the games he played. To say I was a bit disadvantaged was an understatement. I was crushed, broken, tired, disillusioned, embarrassed and scared. And I was too dumb to know just what a predicament I was in. Like the bumblebee that flies only because it doesn't know it's not supposed to, I started out on an incredible flight.

I could type ninety words a minute and in desperation took a job as the sales secretary at WHNT-TV in Huntsville. My degree in Secondary Education and previous school-teaching days in Atlanta meant nothing since I did not have a master's degree. Paying bills and feeding my son, however, meant everything. We lived on $98 (gross) per week in a tiny furnished apartment that came complete with toenail clippings in the shag carpet...someone else's toenail clippings! The first winter, I was so short on money that I kept the thermostat on sixty degrees. We nearly froze to death. My son always remembers.

For two years at WHNT I did the grunt work. What I didn't see then was how lucky I was to be the grunt. I was exposed to training of the best kind in a business that was totally new to me: I learned from the inside out. Certainly, with a college degree, I was overqualified for the job; but I enjoyed it immensely. It was challenging, busy, and a sexy business to be in! The salespeople I worked for soon learned that I could take a load off their shoulders; they learned that I could be trusted; they gave me more and more work to do. And I did it with a smile. I listened more than I talked; I learned to negotiate; I learned to prioritize; I learned to say no; I learned that fair is not equal; I learned that managers are not necessarily leaders and that leaders are a rare breed. I learned to handle seven different people's personalities and quirks. I learned phone skills and the importance of details. I knew my place and always stayed there. I did not gossip.

Then, at the end of year two, my boss offered me a position as a salesperson on straight commission. He had offered this opportunity once before and I had turned him down; his directive was a forceful "now or never." Like a scared rabbit, I said yes and ended up making $19,000 that first year, a huge jump from barely $12,000. From there, the clock started ticking faster than even I can now fathom. I worked my way up to top biller after four years and then was promoted to Local Sales Manager for seven; then for three years to Director of Marketing, where I overcame my horrible fear of computers; then to Vice-President of Sales and Marketing, followed by Station Manager and finally President and General Manager for nine years. It may sound easy, but it spanned a course of twenty-five years and consumed my being. I ended up working longer hours at the top than when I started as a grunt—from 6 A.M. to 6 P.M.—but making a whole lot more than $98 a week!

Those are the facts of my story, but it's the life stuff woven between the facts that etched my leadership style. I was also a wife for the second time and mother to a second child, Natalie. I did dentist appointments, piano lessons, house remodeling, lawn work, tennis lessons, dog tending, cooking, laundry. I was a daughter, a friend, a church worker, a neighbor, a PTA member, a sister, a daughter-in-law. I was exhausted, stretched, bent, occasionally ecstatic, sometimes distraught, never disorganized. I became an expert at multitasking. I learned not to expect any support from a man. I lost another marriage; then joyously fell in love again only to be dismissed by a man I thought was my soul mate. I learned to respect the hurt I saw in other people's eyes; I learned that depression is not a weakness; I learned what it's like to almost lose your daughter to another woman. I learned that grief is stitched into your life fabric. And all the while, I managed millions of dollars; I made dozens of tough decisions a day; I found a wonderful status in the community; I helped others; I served on boards; I learned to pray; I discovered personality flaws like jealousy and control; I met people of the lie who were not fair or honest or stable. I encountered egotism, territorialism, narcissism, dishonesty, defeat, defensiveness. I learned I was tough as nails but fragile as glass. I lived comfortably in my competitive spirit and spread it outward to an entire organization.

I learned that I could survive on almost nothing emotionally and still do my job; I learned to hide my fears and surround myself with great people. I learned to believe in the goodness of people above all else even when they didn't believe in themselves. I learned to be gentle with myself; I learned that a clean house wasn't nearly as important as it had been when I was thirty; I learned to pay people to cook, to clean, to cut grass. I learned how to buy a new car in two hours. I learned that I might have something significant others wanted to hear. I learned that I could be much too candid and much too naïve. I learned that employees wanted my praise more than a raise. I learned that a lot of folks are smarter than I and that people get promoted for all the wrong reasons. I learned to love being number one in a very competitive business.

I found my authentic self. I became a brand of leadership that was an expression of everything I was, everything I stood for, everything I believed in, everything that mattered.

The seed of my leadership style was planted in me years ago by an ethical father and a devoted mother who encircled me in a functional family. It was nourished by church ties and friendships and the idea that trusting others wasn't foolish. It was rooted by high school English teachers who taught me good grammar, good literature, and a love for reading; by math teachers who explained finance, ratios, and fractions; by piano teachers who taught me that I couldn't play certain pieces until I had been in love. It was defined in negative relief by those who were lousy at what they did, who had no respect from their followers, who abused their power and oppressed their subordinates. It flourished in the light of giving credit where credit was due, in being kind to others, in knowing when and how to talk or listen or cry.

I'm nobody famous. I am not rich; I am not previously published; I am not worldly. But I am just like you—a woman who drew upon her very intrinsic makeup to carve out a distinctive leadership style. That is the foundation of this book and the authority upon which the next chapters are based. I earned my way; I carved my path; I shared my glory; I taught all that I knew to others. That's my story and I would bet that much of it is also your story. We have a kinship, you and I, and we haven't even met! Perhaps your leadership role is not as glamorous or your business as sexy as television. Perhaps you won't be quite as lucky as I was. But inside your soul, your process of becoming one of the Leading Ladies is similar because together we share that awesome sense of our femininity.

So with that as a backdrop, spend the next hour with me thinking about your leadership qualities. I am sharing thirty tips out of my story that I believe will make you a dynamic leader. The key ingredient is your femininity! Some of these ideas will hit your radar screen; others will not. My goal is to create a paradigm shift for women in business…suddenly knowing the joy of living and leading as ladies in your own very special female skin!

Chapter 2

The Bad News First

Look carefully before you lead!

These first tips get the bad news out of the way with a dose of realism. They raise the question of why you think you want to be a leader. Your motivation must have absolutely nothing to do with making more money, job security, power, or recognition. Leadership might bless you with these advantages, but true leadership is about courage, risk taking, loneliness, and hard work. It's about denting the environment you manage in such a way that it will be forever different because of your influence.

Take a close, honest look before you proceed onto leadership turf.

Tip #1: Understand the "be/don't be" anomaly

Often, if women reach a level of leadership, it's because they are female. Let me repeat that. Oftentimes, women are promoted just because they are women. Now, before you jump up and down, screaming and ranting, let's be honest! You know it's true; I know it's true; it's just not discussed. It was the case with me—not easy to admit, but I know it in my heart. I'm not bitter about it or dismayed. I was just lucky! I proved to be a good decision and succeeded in leading a television station to a strong, dominant, number one position in the market. But the decision to promote me had everything to do with my company's desire to bring diversity to its core of executives. I was the most likely candidate to bring that goal to fruition. I was in the proverbial right place at the right time. And I thank God I worked for a company with that kind of vision.

My leadership training for the position was pretty pitiful: nothing. But the subtle messages were definitely there: "We're willing to take a chance on you; we think you're good enough to do the job; don't act too much like a woman!!!" I call this the "be/don't be" anomaly. Companies want to bring women to the table, but then they subtly caution us to downplay our femininity.

This is illustrated so well by something that happened to me early on in my new role as CEO. I envisioned that the secret to moving my television station forward from a sluggish number three was to gain prominence in local weather. I wrote an impassioned memo to the higher-ups requesting a quarter-million dollars of capital funding to purchase a Doppler radar for the station, the first in the market. I knew this strategic move was the "kick" that would set us apart and give us the promotional edge we needed. The memo was indeed passionate and put my job on the line for this cause. At the time, my "big boss" was also female. I received a stinging phone call from her and one of the worst reprimands of my career. Her message was loud and clear: "Stop acting like a woman. Don't be so emotional and passionate!" Well, I lost a few inches on my backside to be sure, but we got the Doppler radar in about three months. And it put us on a path to success as our ratings shot up!

After you get where you want to be, leadership tip *numero uno* is to slowly and gently prove to your company that it's absolutely effective and totally appropriate to exercise your femininity. This will not be an easy task.

Warning: Just a quick word of warning. The process only works in the long run if you absolutely know your field. It is the style, not the substance, of your work. You may *get* your promotion to leadership because you are a woman, but you will only *keep* it if you are totally competent.

Tip #2: Get the chip off your shoulder

Quite honestly, I hate those women who are always complaining about how unfairly they are treated. They are cocked and ready to "go off" at even the slightest hint of an insult to their femininity. I attend meetings where you can feel the belligerence, the militant attitude. Women with chips on their shoulders smother any hint of leadership potential. They wear them as badges of courage!

I'm not a hostile female waiting to shoot every man I encounter in business because he might potentially treat me with disrespect. I believe men treat me the way I project myself. I believe that the secret to fair treatment is to expect it, command it, deserve it, and foster it among your organization. I worked for a good company that "got it." So my stories are not horrible. I know there are legitimate cases of sexual discrimination and sexual harassment that must be addressed; I certainly don't mean to downplay them or to devalue those who have been hurt by them. I am suggesting a new way of thinking in regard to this touchy issue.

I was never a "victim," but I could have been if I had chosen to see certain circumstances in a different light. Over the years, I've heard more than my share of dirty jokes, off-color innuendos, and the "good ole boy" crap from high powerful folks in my company. I'm talking about the bad stuff that makes all of our stomachs turn. But instead of threatening to sue over every comment or gesture, I left the scene. I chose to rise above it; never to play into their hands; never to let their immaturity and inappropriateness be a reason to show my colors. You may disagree with this approach, but it works! Men who don't get a reaction leave you alone.

My point quite simply is to expect fair treatment and ignore unfair treatment in lieu of overreacting to it. It's all in how you look through the filter. Be a leader and stay out ahead, not a victim rummaging in the garbage behind. Be proactive, not whiny; be direct, not devious in how you respond in touchy situations. We don't need women who *react* in leadership positions; we need women who *choose to respond* in mature, healthy, steady decisions. Choosing to be treated fairly is probably the most significant choice you will make. As Eleanor Roosevelt so eloquently put it, "No one can make you feel inferior without your consent."

Tip #3: Prepare to be hated

Television is a public business. People know your every move; competition among stations is fierce. Newspapers, God bless them, like to keep it all stirred up; and the "media wars," as they are known, become big discussion around town. Competitive moves are dissected, discussed, dissed, made fun of, second-guessed. I think this is because television is so personal. It is a phenomenon that comes into your home, into dens, bedrooms, even bathrooms. It's your companion; it's how you start your day and many times how you end your day. Anchors become comfortable friends you know. Or that's what we hope for! A passion develops, a sense of ownership. That is all well and good.

So what's the problem? Well, the problem is that because of the intimacy between viewer and station, a scrutiny develops over the leader's decisions. And as always happens, people take sides. Some love you; others hate you. Some support; some criticize. Some applaud; some berate, often brutally. It is no fun to wake up one morning and hear yourself being maligned on talk radio. Or to pick up the newspaper that evening and see your decision as a disparaging headline on the front page.

One of my mentors, Elden Hale, a former officer in the New York Times Broadcast Group and former General Manager, once told me, "If you're not hated, you're not a leader." Well, that seemed like an oxymoron to me at the time. I have come to fully understand. Leaders are out front, doing the cutting-edge stuff. They are thinking outside the box; they are making people stretch; they are often ahead of their time; they are not conformers. If you stake your claim on these turfs, you are going to be hated by some. And if you are not, then I contend you are not a leader.

Our chief meteorologist at WHNT, Dan Satterfield, is a brilliant weatherman, passionate about his business, accurate in his forecasting, and not shy about delivering his message. Huntsville, Alabama, is one of the most tornado-prone areas in the country, and Dan was frustrated by the sluggishness of weather warnings from our local Emergency Management Agency offices during severe weather. Using the best of technology and our new Doppler radar, Dan, with my support, issued tornado warnings when he saw them, many times saving the lives of our viewers. But, as you might guess, the EMA directors weren't fond of this procedure. At one point, we all but had open warfare. This was a dark hour for me as my name and my position won me endless public criticism from this group. But I came to the realization that if I was worth anything at all, I had to stand behind my meteorologist and his ability to predict an oncoming tornado. We decided to put our viewers' safety before the pressure of a government agency. That's what leadership does. It takes the unpopular stand, pursues an uncharted course, and waits out the criticism.

So what does this often unpleasant facet of leadership mean for us women? Well, I believe it means we struggle doubly hard because we generally don't like to be hated. We prefer social acceptance; we like to be liked! We have to accept that it's okay to be hated. Wear it as a badge of courage. Use it as a great lesson in learning not to overreact to criticism. Stand firm; if your decision was the right thing to do before all the negative publicity, then it's the right thing. Don't flounder, don't give in; take your licks; endure the moment. Better they hate you than to ignore you!

Tip #4: Embrace that everything is everyone's job...and that includes you

Every morning after I got to the office, I made a beeline for the coffeepot in the main break room, which was frequently amiss from the night before. I spent the first ten minutes of my day wiping counters and spills on the floor, making coffee, just generally "spiffing up," as we say in the South. My employees never understood why I, the big boss, would do that. Many asked me about it or said, "Oh, Linda, you shouldn't be doing that." The point is they noticed. My reply was always, "Why wouldn't I? I work here, too, and I like for this kitchen to be as clean as mine at home." Leading by example communicated that everything was everyone's job. We all did everything. We did whatever needed to be done, and we did it well.

I asked my employees to work under much stress, to work long hours, to work weekends, to work holidays, to work during times of personal family stress or to miss family celebrations. Couldn't I at least clean the break room, work side by side with them at our weekend events, cheer them on at their baseball games? Couldn't I visit their new babies in the hospital, attend their weddings? Couldn't I walk around when I had time and let them show me what they were doing that day? Couldn't I teach them to job swap, to learn respect for what the other guy did?

No job at our TV station was too small for anyone to do. And no job was positioned with all the glory. We had anchors who helped clean up after parties, engineers who mopped floors when the roof leaked, salespeople who shot footage with news cameras, controllers who wrapped Christmas presents, producers who took up money for T-shirts at expos. You name it, we did it. Little by little, after those walls came down and the doors were opened, we had a ball working and playing together.

Work side by side with your employees...again a trait I believe is a natural one for us women. And, oh yes, if you thought that a leadership position meant working less, breathing a little easier, delegating out all the hard stuff, you are in for a big disappointment!

Chapter 3

"Live It"

All about your philosophy of life

Leaders must first be good people. I have never met a true leader who was dishonest, unfair, operated with poor mental health, or did not have a positive slant on life in general.

True leaders admit their mistakes, value the input of others and expand their outlooks. These tips talk about your philosophy of life and how it impacts your effectiveness in the workplace. If you're unsure about your philosophy, don't even think of heading down the leadership path.

Tip #5: Tell the truth and nothing but the truth

Read the headlines, and they are full of companies and executives who are in trouble for not telling the truth. Lying is a nasty business at any cost, but when the stakes are as high as in big business, you will find yourself in such a quandary of confusion and dismay that your world will tumble down around you. Case in point: the Enron disaster. Tell the truth. No further explanation is necessary! And if your company asks you to do anything else, pack up and leave as fast as you can unplug your laptop. There is no suffering equal to getting caught in illegal corporate crap. I've seen it only from afar, and it has to be the worst set of circumstances I have ever witnessed. And sometimes, good people, good women, because of an element of naïveté, get caught. I'm sorry, but there is no excuse for pleading ignorance. Once you know of misdealings, you are compelled by all the laws of leadership to come forward. Keep your eyes open, your ears clean, and tell the truth! There is a big difference in ladies who lead with integrity and tattletales.

Tip #6: Be competitive but not cruel

Men who sit at the top of their triangles can't afford to be gentle. If they are not good leaders (and many are), they may have to push hard to get down into the organization; they end up squashing the staff's enthusiasm rather than mustering any support for a competitive coup d'état. They have to go in for the kill; they have to impress their male peers in other organizations. They desperately want to win points within their own organizational structure. And the biggie: they don't want to be perceived as a wimp. They often badger and rant and rave, and they take what they want. They aren't into the dance of communication or the awareness of intuition. *Kinder, gentler, softer* would not be adjectives of choice for them. Certainly there are exceptions; I've worked with a few.

Women have a real edge here. I'm the most competitive person you will ever meet, but I'll spin my plan with a smile, not a slap; with a quick turn, not a brutal upheaval; with a savvy, smart, unexpected decision, not a cutthroat maneuver. I as a woman will work on all the people stuff, win the support of the ranks, communicate intently and appropriately, maximize every talent surrounding me, churn the sexy side of promotion and public relations, get all the details aligned, and then I'll zap the hell out of you competitively. And no one will feel mowed down in my organization; no one will get hurt and everyone will gloat in the victory. I can and did win without being cruel and vicious. You as a female can and should use this to your benefit. Perhaps it's another form of that old adage, "kill 'em with kindness."

Actually, I think it goes much deeper than that. To be effective, women have to stay in their natural skin. The competitive traits we possess are mental agility, intuitiveness, charm, communication, openness, cleverness, coyness...am I sounding like a Southern belle? I hope not! We don't have to use cruel and unusual force, make ridiculous demands, dictate unfair tactics, act like a bitch, or disregard the human element to take our organization where we want it to go. We can succeed just as effectively and just as quickly doing it "our" way. The aftermath is that we don't have a bloody battlefield of casualties when we are done. We may have a few Band-Aids to apply but no burials or mutinies.

If you step on your people, those who trust you and look up to you, during a competitive move, you will lose them. It's a very fragile balance. If communicating too much beforehand threatens your move, then for goodness sake, make up for it in the home stretch. Explain, explain, and explain. Factual data dispels gossip and distrust. Including employees in an informative meeting or dialogue waylays their discontent and their ability to compromise your competitive mission downstream. Get them all on your team if you have to meet with every single employee.

Another affiliate in our market spent hundreds of thousands of dollars buying cameras for each employee. And then told the employees to carry the cameras with them wherever they went. At any time, at any venue, during any circumstance of private or public life, they were directed to look for and film news stories. This meant secretaries, salespeople, engineers as well as news personnel. This was an overreaction to our intense competitive moves in the market: our Doppler radar, our helicopter, our additional newscasts, backyard weather, aggressive promotion, and community involvement. This station had been the dominant, number one station for a decade, and suddenly we were a force to contend with. We had made them mad as hell and embarrassed them with first one thing and another. They were fighting for their reputation. Leadership had tried to push the accountability down by forcing employees to be responsible for saving the day. What should have happened was a totally new vision from the thirty thousand–foot level. The employees didn't buy in at all because they were infringed upon and forced to do something inappropriate. The plan failed miserably. It was a desperate, unfeeling strategy, all in the name of being competitive.

Employees will forget almost anything, but they will never forget an inappropriate disregard for their feelings.

Tip #7: Live the Golden Rule unashamedly

Treat others the way you wish to be treated. There is nothing more to say.

Chapter 4

"Do It"

All about your decisions on the job

We can talk style, philosophy, gender differences, etc., till the cows come home. What really defines your report card is what you *do* every day at work. What counts are your methods, your decisions, your actions. This section is the main entrée on the menu for becoming an effective leader. The appetizer and the dessert are important but this is the proverbial "meat and potatoes."

Tip #8: Be a Girl Scout

You learned it just like I did: "Be Prepared"…the Girl Scout motto. You've known it since age twelve probably, but you still haven't quite stitched it into your fabric. Well, now is the time to bring order and preparation to your agenda. If you are unprepared, "they" will eat you alive. Women leaders must use this hopefully innate skill to stay ahead of the game. Why? Because "they" are watching…watching to see if you can do it all and still be a wife and mother; watching to see if children are constantly calling and interrupting your meetings because your home front is disorderly; watching to see if you get flustered and unfocused during the tough times; watching to see if you're as versed as your male counterparts in budgets and capital plans and financial state-ments; watching to see if you can command the respect of your staff; watching to see if you are willing to pull the long hours; watching to see if you can make it look free and easy. Yes, "they" are watching because "they" who promoted you want to look good themselves. And you absolutely *will not* be convincing if you're not prepared.

I can't believe you would be reading this book if you had not gotten this skill down pat. But I know plenty of women in top positions who still run like rats in a maze right before crucial meetings. The days of waiting till the last minute, the days of performing only under extreme deadline, the days of calling frantically on your staff to pull you out of a hole because you're disorganized...those days are over! That was all college behavior. It is not the crux of how women in leadership roles must act. Nobody is impressed when you're unprepared.

Case in point: I recall my first annual budget meeting. I had worked for hours and hours preparing an outline of presentation, going over financial statements, sales figures, budget scenarios for the next five years. I had practically slept with the material under my pillow and been grilled over and over again by my controller. I had stressed considerably over the meeting, anticipated every possible question, knew the whys and wherefores of every expense entry and every capital dollar, tried to make my budget bulletproof. On the day of presentation, I volunteered to be the first of eight general managers to present. I was the only female general manager. I fought hard for over an hour; my budget was heavily scrutinized; the questions came quickly, and I delivered with answers that seemed to work.

The second presenter, a general manager of many years at one of the *New York Times'* other broadcast properties, was a man who admitted that he had nothing prepared. He had jotted down a few quick notes that morning for his presentation, gave a rather flimsy explanation as to what he needed in his budget, rattled on for about ten minutes and passed with flying colors. This is a true story. He wasn't grilled or challenged. Maybe he was smarter than I was; but I don't think so. He was more willing to roll the dice, knowing the ramifications were going to be minimal for him. He had proven success, tenure, and the benefit of being "one of the guys." I was the very first female, on the job for six months and still finding my way into the loop. For me, lack of preparation would have been a stigma long remembered. After I did get tenure and three other female GMs to sit in those meetings with me, I still felt the scrutiny, the separateness. I still felt my style was a bit foreign to the guys. Time took off some of the edge, but the need for preparation, for proving, for precision never waned. I had to excel; I had to be a good choice; I had to stamp my femaleness with a big gold star.

So go home and dig out your Girl Scout Handbook; check the date; realize how long you've been exposed to this orderly directive; start living by it! Be prepared.

Tip #9: Create the communication dance

The very first thing I did as the new president of WHNT was to open the doors. That may sound ridiculously simple and insignificant, but you must understand the situation I inherited. The New York Times Company had blessed us with a new facility, the best in the Southeast for its day. But each department of the station had been closed off by thick, massive, solid oak doors. Employees didn't cross department lines; people didn't know other people's names unless they worked in the same unit. And the general manager's door was always closed. Immediately, I opened all the doors including mine. We bought some fancy, brass doorstops and had at it. Suddenly, I could stand in the hallways and see inside each area of the building. There were real, live people in my organization who had names and hopes and ideas and suggestions to make my job easier. My leadership role was to communicate with them!!

All of us come into the world making sounds. As time goes by, those sounds turn into communication and get more intelligent… hopefully. As time and experience shape us, our tendency is to get on one extreme or the other of the communication loop. We either become too chatty (a female pitfall); or we retreat into an alienating silence (a male pitfall). Yes, I'm generalizing again. Leaders can't afford either extreme. And female leaders, I believe, are blessed with an innate talent for finding the productive middle path. They know how to take their employees by the hand and create a graceful dance of communication. Women usually like to dance, remember! And women love to be in touch! They are not frightened by either gesture.

That door opening signified the start of the dance, at first awkward and shy but eventually a warm, genuine sense of two-way communication, a touching of the minds and spirits. I contend boldly that many men in leadership don't give a damn about communication. In fact, some would say that it leads to problems, that the less the underlings know, the better. If you want the dedication, loyalty, and support of your staff, then listen *and* talk. Know the appropriate moment to do each. Sometimes my employees wanted me to do the talking…telling them exactly what to do firmly, decisively, almost in dictator fashion. Sometimes they needed to ramble through their own mental confusion and finally tell me what was best. That's when I shut up and listened. A good leader senses the path a conversation will take. Sometimes people just need to yell and scream. Sometimes *you* need to yell and scream. Sometimes your silence is all the situation deserves.

I always told my employees that I didn't need their judgment, just their support. But that huge vote of trust can come only after you, as their leader, spend time communicating with them one on one.

Dancing is intimate, special, eye-to-eye behavior. So is communicating!

Tip #10: Be there...and be fair

A television station runs 24/7, 365 days a year. It doesn't stop for deaths, birthdays, anniversaries, or holidays and often gets busier when the rest of the world comes to a halt. Think of September 11, 2001. People in the TV business were not sitting at home with their families in shock and mourning watching CNN. No, broadcasting is in many ways a rather nasty business. Because of that, it's vital that the leader of the ship be ever visible. In a twenty-four–hour operation, I couldn't interact with the folks who come in at 4:30 in the morning unless I was around for part of their shift. I couldn't get to know my weekend staff unless I showed up in the building on the weekends. Pretty simple!

Women again have a knack for this "motherly" sense of just being around. Checking in, looking over shoulders, asking questions, caring about what's happening to people. Women aren't made for exclusive ivory towers. They don't sit well behind closed doors. Maybe we're just nosy by nature; we want to see what's going on. I made sure to see every shift at least once a week, hopefully every day. I got up at 4:30, was at work by 6 A.M. and left at 6 P.M. That was a long, hard day; but for me, it was the only choice I had. How can you lead people you never see?

In that vein of being visible and being present, be even. Play no favorites. Ask any mother and she'll tell you that she loves her children the same. If she doesn't, she's not a good mother. Some kids require more attention than others because of circumstances; some employees do too. But that's a discussion for the case of Fair vs. Equal. Read on.

Tip #11: Understand that "fair" is not always "equal"

A local car dealer taught me a valuable truism years ago when I was new to sales and called on him for advertising. I call it the "Fair is not equal" rule. He explained it this way:

"Two people come into my dealership to buy cars. One is a brand new customer; the other has bought five cars from us in previous years. We're appreciative of both; but the previous customer will get more attention, quicker resolution and more price negotiation than the new customer. Each will be treated fairly; but that treatment will not be equal because of the difference in circumstances."

I realize that any of us could shoot holes in the theory, but I'm here to convince you that this explanation works extremely well in dealing with employees. Every situation involves its own set of distinctive circumstances, and those conditions must be looked at when deciding how to treat an employee. Employees are fond of screaming, "That's not fair!" To which we can reply, "Yes, it's fair; it's just not equal. Let me explain the difference!"

I taught my employees that difference, and it was helpful many times in settling disputes and controversy. Case in point. One of my department heads frequently left early on Fridays around 3 P.M. Another employee loved to cry foul about this openly. He finally came in to me demanding to know if I was aware this person was leaving early. I had granted the permission for the early exits—in fact, encouraged them. I conveyed this fact and made it clear that the situation was really none of his concern. He continued to moan that it wasn't fair because he had to stay until five o'clock. (Here's where you can use the rule and your very effective communication skills.) I explained softly *and with a smile* that the woman who left early had also worked every night that week on a special project and that she generally worked almost every weekend at events for the station. Then I asked the grumbler if he would like to put in all those extra hours each week; that halted the discussion.

The grace, the perk, the exception you give to one employee may not be equal in comparison; but it most assuredly can be fair. Fair is not always equal. It's a good life rule in any business. Small, narrow minds want equality. Mature, understanding minds appreciate fairness. Leaders must know the difference. Female leaders can use the communication dance here to reap a very productive outcome.

Tip #12: Slay the dragons

Women have a tendency to keep everyone happy. It's a trait we learned from our mothers. In the workplace, this is impossible. You cannot lead and keep everyone happy. Conflicts arise daily, most quite small and easy to handle. The big ones test our true dynamic. Failing to deal with conflict will bite your effectiveness and water down your respect from employees. Slay your dragons quickly and decisively. Make the worst thing you have to do for the day the first thing on your list. Get it off your radar screen as soon as possible. I believe in three meetings to handle internal conflicts:

1. Identify the players in a conflict and meet with each separately. Document their input.
2. Meet with anyone who was a witness to the conflict and get his or her data and document it.
3. Meet with the opposing parties together and expose the data you've collected.

That is really pretty simple and it works. It avoids the "she said that he said that they said" runaround. Step number four is to follow up a month later to see if the conflict has subsided. Of course, the last and most important step for you is to document, document, document. Corporate legal will love you!

A Footnote: Your company should have a policy and procedures manual for such issues as harassment, email violations, etc.

Make sure you are thoroughly schooled in the fine points; always have a witness present for discussions on controversial issues.

Tip #13: Know how to hire and when to fire

We've established clearly, I hope, that as women, we're blessed with great communicative and intuitive skills. So use them to put the best possible team in place. And you do that by hiring only "your kind of people" and getting rid of those who aren't. It will take you a while to know the latter. Develop a real finesse for the interview process; come up with a profile of the team player you want; benchmark against that set of criteria and let nothing steer you away. Prepare to fire (within the processes of your organization) all of those people who fall outside your profile. You can remake most of them, but not all. If they stand between you and success, you will get tired of going around them. And then a strange thing will happen: they will take ownership of their ability to make you go around them. Then they've got you; you'll spend precious leadership time dealing with unnecessary employee relations.

I recall a director we'll call Hank who was excellent in his job but had a terrible habit of using the "F" word when he got upset during a live newscast. The "F" word was grounds for termination with our company, especially after multiple warnings had been issued. Hank knew he was too good to be fired; he knew we would step around him; but I knew he was going to get a harassment suit claim against him if things didn't change. I asked our attorney to come over one afternoon. I put him in the conference room with Hank for about two hours. My instructions were, "Put the fear of God into him or else I'm going to have to fire him. Tell him in plain English what can happen if a woman is offended by his comments and brings charges. Tell him about humiliation and jail and losing his job, etc." I didn't go in the room but something worked and Hank stopped making us work around him. We also sent him to an anger management class.

Hire carefully; fire quickly. If you're good, you will know in sixty to ninety days who to keep, who to let go, and what kind of team member you are most looking for. *Personnel selection is the top skill a good leader must have.* If you've got slugs on your team who hold you back, don't blame them; blame yourself.

Here are a few of my favorite open-ended interview questions for the hiring scene:

1. What would your co-workers say about you if I could meet with them today?
2. What would your present boss say about you?
3. What is your greatest weakness? Your greatest strength?
4. Why, above all other candidates, should I give you the job?

These aren't brilliant questions but notice that they have nothing to do with money, availability, aptitude (which is presumed), or background. They have to do with the quality of person who will become a team member in your organization. And, yes, by the way, we've all been wrong about people we've hired. I hired and fired a salesperson (female) in the scope of five days, and let a main female anchor go after one month! I knew they were mistakes. Don't let those linger, even if it's embarrassing to have been so wrong. Be appropriate and be legal. But be determined to get them out of your organization.

Tip #14: Trust your intuition

Books have been written on women's intuition. A web search produced 22,271 points of reference. Must be something to it! It works in several ways to our benefit.

Our body is an intuitive caution light. Pay attention to a knot in your stomach, a rush of blood to your face, sweaty palms, increased heart rate, a queasy sense of unsteadiness. Your body will absolutely tell you when something is not quite right or someone is not quite on the up and up. Don't be forced or persuaded to act when your body sounds an alarm! Every time I blew by that twinge in my gut, I got burned or made a bad decision. Then I would beat myself up horribly and lament the worst dilemma of all—regret. Check out each and every twinge. Do your homework. Perhaps there'll be nothing to it; but oh, the joy of saving yourself all that trouble.

A quick story. One of our female anchors moved to get married, and we quickly went in search of a replacement. One particular candidate looked good on paper and looked good on the exterior, which quite candidly is important for any anchor. Interviewing usually included a dinner. We met at a local restaurant. When the waiter came for her order, she took a good fifteen minutes to decide. My body signs were screaming and my intuitive "What's this?!!!" was raging. I watched in horror as she changed her mind about six times. That tiny inner voice said, "Don't go there, Linda. This gal's bad news." However, over the course of the next two days, I allowed my news director to talk me out of my gut feelings. I hired her despite my misgivings. We promoted the bejesus out of her, including outside press coverage, etc., etc., etc. I watched with horror as all of my concerns quickly materialized in living color. In exactly thirty days, I swallowed all of my pride and made the cardinal exposure of stupidity. I took her off the air, terminated her employment, and somehow sidestepped a contract without legal ramifications. There is no grief like that of blowing past your gut.

Intuition is also your best ally in meetings. I have closed my door after many a meeting to ask an employee who attended the same meeting if they "sensed" this or that. Most often, no one "got it" but me. The "it" was a sense of the undercurrent of personality, the innermost thoughts bouncing around the room, the tensions, the jealousies, the personality conflicts. I could feel that odd sense of awareness and used it to set up the communication dance we were just talking about. Some might call it reading people; I call it gut intuition. I believe it is a gift that most women have in large doses.

Keep a record of your intuitive success rate. I have done that for years. I'm batting almost a thousand in the gut department. My employees learned to listen when I told them that a particular decision, situation, person didn't "feel right." They respected my gut check, and we were always ahead of the game.

Tip #15: Have a male devil's advocate

Many of my best employees were men; many of my business peers were men, and many of my dearest friends are men. With such constant male interaction, I was always aware of how different the male approach was from mine. I could tell what men were thinking and found it fascinating to watch them. I learned to use their expertise at every turn and to examine their thinking patterns. I tested ideas on them; I watched their interpretations to new processes, to conflict, to change. I watched and I used their input to determine strengths and weaknesses of my business plans. After I stirred their assessment with a teaspoon of my own femininity, I made my decision and took action. Some men often thought my decisions bordered on the ridiculous. They thought some of what I did was flippant and unnecessary, too soft, too risky, too quick, too off-road, too altruistic. But I was the boss; they weren't; and they learned a new way. Slowly we took over the market, and it became hard to argue with success.

One key part of this process is having a male devil's advocate on your team. If you don't have one by natural default, appoint one. Men understand the "king of the mountain," "winner take all" approach; women favor win/win approaches. You will need someone to delineate these different styles, question every decision you make; someone to be the naysayer, the skeptic, the watch guard to point out how another man will respond and view your decisions. After all, in many situations, your competitive peer will be male.

My devil's advocate was my Director of Operations, a department head and vice president of the unit named Dick Wright. He was a brilliant guy, knew everything about television, but tended to be very rigid in his thinking and in his decisions. He's the kind of right arm you wanted around but very much the scrutinizing skeptic and naysayer.

In 1993, a nasty issue was thrust upon broadcasters and cable companies, and Dick was the lead dog on this project. Television stations tried to get cable companies to pay them money in exchange for signal carriage. As you might suspect, things became adversarial in a hurry. I thought it was all a waste of time. Cable companies weren't going to pay us any money, and we weren't going to stand by and let the cable companies take us off their systems, which was their only recourse if we pushed them to the wall. I wanted to do other things instead of asking for money: promotional inserts in their billing statements, news promos on their various channels, local news cut-ins on their channels, etc. It was a softer, gentler approach than demanding money. I invited each cable operator into my conference room and together we worked out some very clever deals, none of which had hard dollars involved. Dick thought me a little crazy at the outset. He wanted more; he wanted money; he wanted to show them who was right, who had the power. He was invaluable to me in all the knowledge he possessed about the market, and he did all the daily grind, all the research and paperwork. I watched and listened intently to his suggestions, reactions, predictions, but forged my own path. We accomplished a string of partnerships rather than declaring war. "Everyone wins" worked much better than "winner take all." And in the end Dick agreed that we had pulled off a magnificent list of victories.

Toward the end of my career, I discovered the impact of my leadership on the men I had managed. At my retirement party, first one and then another shared a touching story of how *my* leadership had affected *their* lives. I was thanked for demanding only the best, for caring about their personal lives, for pushing them hard, for recreating a sense of pride, for being fair, for being visible, for showing them how to work as a team, for building a family atmosphere. What a night for me. What a promise of hope for you!

Tip #16: Motivate the team

As soon as I was made president of the television station, I was faced with the daunting task of trying to forge a team out of a group of discouraged and dysfunctional department heads who had lost their soul, their identity, and their focus. They were distrustful, undermining of each other, and very territorial. "Team" was not in their vocabulary. A lack of direction had sucked all the life out of them. Slowly, day by day, they discovered the magic of working together, tearing down walls, trusting, focusing on the whole instead of the individual parts.

Now I wasn't anyone special, but I did understand how to motivate people by using those feminine skills that come naturally. I was able to capitalize on a rarely tapped facet of the human soul: surfacing a conviction that did not want to disappoint either me, their leader, or each other.

What I did is a pretty simple three-step process. I could do it only by getting my own ego out of the way, something which men have a harder time doing in my opinion. The steps go like this:

1. **Tell people they can do it** (whatever "it" is). Preach, inspire, excite, invigorate, applaud! Also, while you're playing the cheerleader, create structures, lay out expectations, don't allow misbehavior or old patterns. HAVE A PLAN as only a woman can do!

2. **Let them do it.** Don't do their jobs for them. Delegate and wait. Stand by their side and watch. Be there for whatever the mundane tasks are as a helper, but let them run their show. Not only do they *not* want to disappoint you, but they quickly see your total reliance on their ability to breed success or embarrassing failure.

3. **Tell them they've done it.** And this means whether good or bad. Immediate feedback is the key. Give great applause and credit for a job well done. But just as importantly give immediate feedback on errors, failure, poor judgments. This is much harder to communicate but actually more necessary and

more effective. It's the way to keep the standard of excellence alive and well in the team. Allow other team members to give feedback as well.

Bottom line is that you drive and steer the horses, but with time let them do all the work. At the end of the day, everyone is tired but can collectively celebrate where you've come. In summary do it all as a group:

♦ Group ownership
♦ Group celebration
♦ Group grief
♦ Group support around a problem
♦ Group problem solving
♦ Group goal setting

The last piece of this motivation miracle is that when you are down, the team will motivate you! And thus you can become a self-fulfilling prophecy! It is truly amazing what the human spirit can do when motivated to act as a team.

Tip #17: Learn that business is business and friends are friends

Never, I repeat never, socialize with your business associates, especially those you manage and lead each day. Performance evaluations should be based on performance, not friendship. If you mix the two, your perspective will become tainted and the employee will be totally confused. You can't drink beer together on Thursday night and then lower the boom on Friday morning at nine o'clock for a project that went awry. For lack of a better adjective, it just gets "messy." Business must be clean and clear. Save the social times for friends totally outside of work, especially a covey of good girlfriends. I think even your home should, for the most part, be off-limits. Employees invariably think their pay is inferior and inadequate, and seeing your gorgeous, well-appointed home will do nothing but foster this gap. Stay a bit mysterious on the personal side.

Tip #18: Stand pretty close to the water fountain but don't drink

Water cooler conversation is the weekly gossip around your workplace. It is absolutely vital that you know what is being said, by whom, and about whom. You certainly don't want to engage in the chatter directly or necessarily believe everything that you hear. But hear it you must to stay online and informed. Most of it is worthy of full-blown disregard, but every now and again, a tidbit will float your way that must be addressed. Employees have a way of knowing what is *really* going on. Surprises can mean trouble, time, and embarrassment for you.

Over the years, I learned who was looking for another job, who was having an affair with whom, who was calling corporate with bad information, who was spreading misinformation about other employees, who was rallying forces against a certain idea, who was getting a divorce, who was coming in late every day, who was complaining about new initiatives, etc., etc. Certainly, some of this was none of my business. But the essence of the information more than the facts often provided insight in dealing with situations and people as they performed their jobs, which was my business.

You are expected to know everything. Make sure you do.

Tip #19: Emote!

If you work crossword puzzles, you know this word! One of the things I did with my employees was to express emotion.

We worked our behinds off to gain dominance in the Nielsen ratings. That's the only report card a television station gets, certainly not a perfect process, but the only one available. That rating book was our lifeline to revenue. Most folks forget that an over-the-air broadcaster does not charge a penny for services. That's your cable or satellite provider. We existed off revenue from advertising only, and low ratings meant low revenue. When we got our ratings in, if they were good, there was joy and celebration throughout! And I was the main cheerleader. I had one dear male employee who would never show one drop of emotion on ratings delivery day. He never jumped up and down, never hugged a fellow employee, never did a high-five, never ordered a cake to celebrate, never beamed from ear to ear. He "contained" himself.

Well, I'm here to suggest that containment is not what works with everyday, hardworking people. They love to see you, as their leader, pleased with a good report card. Celebrate with them! Let them see the pleasure in your face; walk the halls; order pizza and throw a quick party; emote...emote...emote. Let that wonderful passion come out. You better believe that we women can do this one better.

Chapter 5

"Sell It"

All about your style

Think about meeting someone for the very first time. You will probably not remember names or companies (unless you are exceptionally well trained in this skill). You'll be more likely to remember their outstanding features, how they are groomed, or some personality trait. It is their essence which will leave a first impression.

Leaders, especially female leaders, understand the power of essence.

Tip #20: Wear buttons and bows

Why does business attire have to be straight out of a nunnery? Why can't we just be ourselves expressing appropriately in fashion and accessories our personality and zest for life? If we're learning to successfully survive in the male world, why in the world would we choose to wear what turns men off? Why would we de-emphasize our wonderful powers of being feminine? The answer is simply beyond me! To all who advocate conservative, safe, inconspicuous, dull, I'd suggest you look at yourselves in the mirror.

I love wonderful clothes and spent a great deal of money building a power wardrobe. But it's not like any power wardrobe you've ever seen before. I wore red and zany purple paisley and orange and animal prints and boots and snappy linen blazers! I wore what felt comfortable for the day, the mood, the occasion. I didn't want to evaporate into the background; I wanted to stand out and be noticed. My clothes were a statement of my leadership vision: bold, daring, risky, and unconventional.

I discovered that my employees actually loved to see me dress smartly. It connoted success to them, made them feel proud, and they frequently told me so. In fact, when I retired, I had a female anchor try to negotiate for my suits! I was flattered. It's not about what you wear; it's about whether you are comfortable with yourself in what you wear and positioned to represent your company with confidence. Know your comfort zone internally, not what you've been conditioned to believe is politically correct.

Here are some new fashion rules for the new millennium... according to no one but me!

1. Wear the best that you can afford.
2. Focus on great, sexy shoes and matching stockings. Remember the two out of three rule. Shoes, stockings, and skirt should all match in color; or if not, at least two out of three.
3. Use scarves to add softness, classic hair accessories to hold back long hair.
4. Wear a perfume that suits you and wait for the compliments. People will definitely notice! Don't change after the compliments start coming. Your fragrance will linger long after you have gone. Make it light, soft and very feminine. My favorite is a Pear Essence that you can buy almost anywhere.
5. Wear pearls and pretty pins; go easy on the sparklies unless they are real diamonds!
6. Bright colors are great if they're the right colors for you. Have a color analysis done.
7. Don't forget regular manicures and haircuts. You can afford it now! If you want to hide your fingers under the table during that important presentation, you're in trouble.

8. Don't wear high-maintenance outfits that you are constantly tugging and pulling at. Make it simple, well groomed, well-fitting. You want to be conspicuous but not self-conscious.
9. No runs in stockings…ever!
10. Wear bright red lipstick…men love it.

Clothes make the woman in business just like they make the man. Be bold but never suggestive. Show off the best body part you have—neck, legs, height, hair. Play to your strengths and you'll be amazed at the results. People will remember you, your name, your firm, what you do. Your very "presence" becomes your calling card!

First I was Linda; then I was the CEO. I never got those roles reversed. You shouldn't either. I'm telling you to undo some of what you've been told about being a blah, genderless nothing. Leaders are never blah! Be bold and distinctive in your wardrobe and watch how others will respond to you in amazing ways.

Tip #21: Squawk like a mother hen

Hover, pick, pester, swoop around, remind, leave Post-it notes, leave voice mails, leave emails, page, call in from home, call in when traveling if you want things to run well both in your presence and in your absence. I do believe it's a womanly thing by nature to do the details. Most men absolutely will not be bothered because they have a wife at home and a secretary at work who does the details for them!

Living with the minutiae isn't sexy or fun; however, slipping into a state of sloppiness and disorganization will be much worse. Your "mother hen" role is guaranteed to drive your employees a little crazy for a while; then it will dawn on them that, by damn, she expects things to be right.

"God is in the details" was one of our mottos. And my employees with time and training and persistence began to get it right the first time, just to keep me off their backs. It's behavior modification by pestering to death. It works! Employees will eventually come to joke with you about it, and in the process you will achieve a level of excellence that will knock everyone's socks off!

A quick story. My pet peeve at the television station was misspelled words that made it to air. I would page abruptly and loudly over the loudspeaker during a newscast identifying the error and calling for immediate correction. Three things happened. First of all, my employees couldn't believe I was still in the building; second, they realized that I was actually watching the product that was their day's work; and third, that I had caught the error. The message: Far better to run spell check next time than to have me on their backs, pecking away like a mother hen. I'm telling you, it works!

You may find this tip somewhat unbecoming; you may think that employees should behave independently without being reminded of all the details. You shouldn't have to be a mother hen. You can think that if you wish. I believe you must set the bar high; you must stress the particulars; you must enforce accountability by acting in ways at first that get their attention. Only then, over time, can you breed a level of independent excellence. And after you do, you'll have much more time to lead…to vision, to plan, to strategize. There will be much less need to do the squawking. Teach your employees that you are paid to think; they are paid to do—so that you have time to think. That is not demeaning; it is simply efficient. Teach them that you wish to be spared the details! This takes time and trust and some squawking at first.

Most of your employees will fly around five thousand feet; your perspective must soar like a visionary to the thirty thousand–foot level. Have a great flight!

Tip #22: Use a soft touch

Just as a woman can light up a party, we can also lighten up the workplace. We can do what comes so naturally for us. Women are the family makers. We have the soft touch. We know of such things as weddings, babies, funerals, divorces, diamond rings, broken hearts, dentist appointments, and runny noses. We know and we understand because we've lived the dramas; we've done the details.

I am boldly suggesting, in fact *insisting*, that if we take this distinct gender and cultural advantage into the workplace...if we use our special sensitivity and awareness with an even, gentle touch, we can get our employees to love us. And when people know we really care about them, they do not want to disappoint us. They will go to the far ends of the earth for us to get the job done the way we want it done. They will absolutely do amazing feats to get our pat on the back, a high five, or a brief moment of our recognition. Forget about what we pay them; they want our stroke, our acknowledgment, our blessing on their performance.

Don't forget to ask about sick kids, a spouse who's been laid off, a girlfriend who's having surgery, a "Happy Birthday" or the most prized possession of all, a handwritten note or card. Throw out some grace to that employee who's going through a divorce (we've been there!), who's just moved into a new house, who has a kid just diagnosed with autism. Put yourself in their shoes and feel what it would mean to have an understanding, accommodating supervisor. Then express those feelings to your employees. Many men have the awareness, but many don't know how to express it or just won't.

Have a game plan for your employees' highs and lows:

♦ Understand, expect and plan for some degree of low productivity around the Christmas holidays.
♦ Keep a stash of cards for every occasion, and take time to write those short personal notes.
♦ Listen for details about your employees' lives.
♦ Watch for a change in demeanor or a depressed countenance, a slow movement in a usually lively person, a distant look in the eyes—all sure signs of depression.
♦ Speak frequently and with confidence about your Employee Assistance Program. Have a private chat with an employee to

suggest he or she use the resources of counseling available to employees. Don't be afraid to talk from personal experience!

Put simply, learn the dialogue of "personal." You already know it because you can feel it. Learn to act on it, albeit in a professional manner. For goodness' sake, act on it. It's one of those God-given attributes that we have as women. Don't work hard to bury, harden or minimize your best chance to win the devotion of your staff.

We've all known some men and maybe some women who would say all of this personal stuff is baloney. "You can't run a business this way. People are not your family members; job comes first, personal stays at home." To this I say an absolute, strong-arm, proven "Bah, humbug!" However, be prepared amid total sincerity on your part for some employees to abuse your kindness, take advantage of your understanding, and worst of all play tit-for-tat with you. They will compare what you did for them to what you did for others and expect exact treatment to prevail. Here's the "Fair is not equal" discussion again. These obstacles are, in my opinion, not good enough reason to abstain from being naturally female with your workforce.

I can't end this chapter without reminding you that as you go about being all the leading lady you can be, *you cannot expect a 100 percent return.* You are simply using your softer side, your feminine strengths, to create an atmosphere that produces a highly productive work environment. Employees come and go—retire, transfer, resign—but you will hopefully remain. What counts in the long run is the reputation that surrounds you.

The most wonderful words I ever heard from my staff were, "Linda really cares about the people who work here." They also knew in the same thought process that I would kick their ass for a sloppy job. It doesn't get any better than that!

Tip #23: Run like a deer

Run! Don't walk. There's nothing worse in my opinion than a sluggish, droopy woman walking down her own halls. It connotes no excitement, no energy, no zest for the job. What's even more effective is to run in your heels so they click against an uncarpeted floor if one exists in your workplace. Your employees will know you are close by! Run so that nobody can catch you. Lee Iacocca's famous line, "The speed of the boss is the speed of the team" hung in my office as a reminder to be out in front of everyone else.

This may sound absolutely absurd to you, but it is one of the traits which endeared me to my employees and became a piece of my legacy. The symbolism of moving quickly, of being out in front, of letting your presence be known, of having a distinctive sound that belonged only to you, of being focused in a certain direction—all great assets for a leader.

Tip #24: Smile ☺

My best physical asset is my smile. This is often the case for women. I used it all the time, as natural as sunlight, to awaken cooperation, to dispel argument, to breed loyalty, to instill trust, to teach by example, to win hearts to a passion that I needed for victory. It was a daily pep rally. So…use your smile. It's the only free capital asset you have and comes with no tax or depreciation schedule!

Chapter 6

Taking Care of Yourself

All about preserving your energy

L eaders run full steam ahead all their waking hours. How in the world can you maintain that level of energy without some self-rejuvenation? It must be deliberate, regular and coveted. Nothing gets in the way of "your" time for you. Women do carry an extra burden here because society and culture have mapped a route for us as wives and mothers. These tips are some of the most important in the book. Commit to them.

Tip #25: Find a good wife

For the first three years of my daughter's life, I had a full-time nanny, housekeeper, cook, and secretary, all in one. She even bought my groceries! It was heaven. I went home able to enjoy the precious little time I had with my baby. Unfortunately, I could not sustain that situation, but it taught me the importance of giving myself permission to use outside resources to lessen my stress.

Quit trying to be Superwoman. Admit you need a little help. I always threatened to run an ad in the local classifieds for a good wife. Even if you are blessed with a supportive husband (I wasn't), you will be overwhelmed by all the boiling pots that are spilling over in your daily life. I highly recommend finding an outside assistant/nanny/housekeeper to take care of the home front: laundry, homework, dry cleaning, dentist appointments, braces, transportation, food preparation, pest control folks, etc. By this time in your career, you can afford it. Someone should start a business called Wives for Women and turn it into a national franchise!

Tip #26: Wear the coat without those designer labels!

A woman in a leadership position should understand the leadership coat, as I call it. When you cross the threshold of ultimate responsibility, you wear a new set of clothes, made out of the fabrics of maturity and good mental health. There is no room for poutiness, hurt feelings, paranoia, jealousy, resentment, gossip— all stereotypically female. These traits give credence to that nasty label, "the weaker sex." Absolutely none of that! Learn to conduct business with all the positive feminine strengths you have; store up the weaknesses for downtime away from the workplace. You can have an occasional pity party, but have it at home. Cry big alligator tears every once in a while, but do it over an evening glass of wine...at home. Never share your internal "stuff" with an employee you are managing. That's not being feminine; it's being stupid. Showing positive emotion is wonderful; acting out PMS or menopausal mania isn't!

If the stakes get really high and the stress is beating you down (like the time my female anchor was sent before a judge for owning a strip club!), go for a walk around the block at work. Settle your emotions, clear your head, move your body until the haze has cleared. Return to the office and do business. Never stoop to the antics some of your employees pull on you. We fly at thirty thousand feet and sit in First Class. Don't forget it!

Tip #27: Meditate

I'm not talking about regurgitating anything to do with work. I'm talking about soul business. Work on *you*. Be quiet; be still; know your inner values; know whom you worship; know what you worship; know what you are grateful for; know your weaknesses and your strengths; look at yourself in the mirror. Examine; expand; evaluate; edify; enlarge; envelope; engulf; engage—all of this with just yourself! The entire rest of your day will be spent with other people, problems, decisions, dilemmas, frustrations, successes, failures, meetings, deadlines, email, phones, pages, cancellations, disappointments. The list could go on and on. For God's sake, for your sake, take fifteen precious moments for yourself and be at peace.

Buy a copy of *Simple Abundance: A Daybook of Comfort and Joy* by Sarah Ban Breathnach and read it daily if you need a guide, a structure. Find *at least* fifteen minutes of quiet time away from another living soul and recharge your batteries. Don't tell me that you can't. You can! Get up earlier, get to work earlier, go to bed later, take a lunch break, sneak out for a walk (you're the boss, remember!). But find time specifically to meditate. You can make it a religious experience if you wish. You can pray, you can hum, you can do yoga, but do something in peace and quiet, just for yourself. Your quest is to meet your authentic self, a person you may not even know yet!

And yes, I contend that successful career women do this more easily than their male counterparts. Men finally arrive when they are a bit older and mellower, when the competitive juices have given way to golf courses, gardens, and grandchildren...when the wrinkles on their faces no longer bother them and the extra wifely pounds they snuggle with at night don't really matter. As women, we can be ahead in the soul game because we aren't afraid to look inward at a much earlier age.

Tip #28: Get physical

That's it. Get physical. Walk, dance, play golf, play tennis, do yoga, join a fitness spa, swim, ski, hike, do housework, mow the grass, skate, bike, garden—whatever best suits you. No excuses, no delays. Just do it! *If you don't have your health, you have nothing.*

My personal favorite recommendation is to learn to play golf. It requires a singularity of focus; it will allow no other gods before it. It requires a commitment of time that removes you from the rat race long enough to settle yourself. You can't think about work or home, all the things you did or didn't do, *and* play golf at the same time. The mental discipline is intense. The physical practice is brutal. You become consumed beyond your present mental state, and slowly the stress dissolves. You have found your quiet spot in the world amid the beauty of nature, interesting people, wonderful travel opportunities, and potential new friendships. And remember, women play golf for totally different reasons than men do. Men play to win; women play to find some inner soul peace. What a delicious feminine difference!

Chapter 7

The Final Layer

All about perspective

Perspective comes with maturity, with time spent, with lessons learned, with success under our collars and failures tightly woven into our experience. These tips are where you will naturally go if you've really achieved leadership at its most fulfilling level.

Tip #29: Beware the corporate sinkhole

Corporations have a way of turning us into slices of white bread — all the same, all neatly tucked away in a conforming package with the same consistency and texture. The worst epitaph I could have on my tombstone would be, "Here lies Linda, a leader who got sucked into mediocrity." If you work for a large corporation as I did, you will face the daily challenge of holding your own individuality, of standing for what you believe is good for your arm of the company, of standing up to the brownnosers, the wannabes, the tattletales. You will always be encouraged to ride the middle, play it safe, not rock the boat, and not make anyone above you look bad.

I'd sooner quit than be mediocre. The corporate sinkhole as I like to call it catches you in a swirl and can suck you under. Managing upward is tricky. I wish you good luck; this was not my best skill because I'm far too candid, far too determined, far too clear on what is best. Balance is the key between keeping your job and keeping your sense of integrity over leadership issues.

Sadly, doing what is right from a leadership perspective may not always blend with the goals of your company. Have a good, solid mentor of either gender who can help you sort things out. But unfortunately, do not put total trust in anyone with whom you work. Trust yourself and that's about it! Naïveté here can really cause you some problems. The person in your company who will side with you over his/her own job security is one in a million. Don't ask people to choose. The very first page of this book told you that leadership turf is a lonely place! Stand ready to fight your battles alone. And if you can't stand the heat, get out of the fire. There's always another company looking for dynamic leadership.

Tip #30: Exit before the curtain falls

Exit the stage before the curtain falls on you. Timing is everything in knowing when to stay and when to leave a company. Know when to get out. Always leave when you're on top. Exit gracefully like the lady you are, whether it is to retire or to take the next challenge. And by all means, take a bow; you deserve it! If you have been a dynamic leading lady, the applause will ring in your ears for years to come.

Bonus Tip: Leave a legacy

Stephen Covey has a wonderful passage in his book *The Seven Habits of Highly Effective People* where he talks about attending your own funeral and hearing what others have to say about you. I contend that leading ladies leave legacies that people speak about for years to come. After you are gone, employees will remember your smile, the communication dance, the demand for perfect details, the smell of your cologne, the conflict that you handled well, the clicking of your heels, the difference between fair and equal. Because you are a woman, they will remember the fashion statement you always made, the warmth of your presence, the soft side that touched their personal lives. You've taught them how to excel, how to expect more of themselves and each other; you've taught them how to celebrate victory, how to endure defeat, how to respect co-workers, how to reach for good mental health. You must leave a legacy of legitimate behavior in a workplace that might otherwise be torn by stress, tension, and mundane mediocrity. Employees will long be affected by the essence of your character, and there is no responsibility as great as that one.

Consider your legacy as you go along. Know how you want to be remembered. It will be a steady benchmark by which to gauge your own daily performance. It's wonderful to think that my employees miss me, but more than that, I'd like to think that they thrive on a commitment to excellence because of something I left on their mental doorsteps.

Postscript: Where Do Good Leaders Go?

Leaders don't die, and they don't just fade away; they reinvest, taking their talents to the community. Once a leader, always a leader. Leadership doesn't wash off; the responsibility to serve doesn't disappear when you retire unless of course health considerations are a factor.

My retirement has been the richest time of my life. I awake with a smile on my face and more commitments on my calendar than at any time before. I mentor young women who need a shove in the right direction; I serve on boards for both profits and nonprofits that need the expertise of quality business judgment. I care for my elderly mom. I provide loving leadership still, I hope, to my children. And yes, every once in a while, I just play!!

For some wonderful reason, God chose me to be a leader. I will choose always to live that role with every ounce of energy I possess.

Godspeed on your leadership journey!

Are you looking for a motivational speaker?

Ms. Spalla is available for speaking engagements to clubs, civic groups, and churches and offers half-day seminars for businesses regarding the leadership skills highlighted in *Leading Ladies*. For information concerning speaking arrangements, please check her Web site at www.lindaspalla.com.

For information on purchasing additional copies of this book, contact Linda Spalla at

      P.O. Box 4047
      Huntsville, AL 35815-4047
      Fax: 1-888-895-3756

Or order online at www.lindaspalla.com